I0140992

BEAUTIFUL
A Broken Little Tale

Written

and

Illustrated

by

Mar García-Amorena Plana

BEAUTIFUL
A Broken Little Tale

Copyright 2017 Mar García-Amorena Plana

All rights reserved.
No part of this book may be used
or reproduced in any manner whatsoever
without written permission except
in the case of brief quotations embodied
in critical articles and reviews.

ISBN 978-0-9903823-4-8
Library of Congress Control Number: 2017915912

Editing by Ruth Beach

Printed in the United States of America

First Printing December 2017

Sunny Day Publishing, LLC
Cuyahoga Falls, Ohio 44223
www.sunnydaypublishing.com

SUNNY DAY®
PUBLISHING, LLC

This book is a warm

hug to all those

compulsive,

misunderstood,

fierce,

beautiful minds.

You are valid.

You are

perfect.

Like the Wolf loves

the Moon, my love.

There is a forgotten
little story about a
girl who had a secret
to protect.

Her mind was a
strange place,
full of brambles
and tricky paths.

She was precious,
because she was a storm.

A thunderstorm.

When she got upset
or sad,
dark clouds
appeared above her
and vented fury
all around.

She was
fierce,
destructive,
and somehow
graceful.

And she was always alone.

One day,
she started walking.
Her steps were slow
and light.
She was looking
for something she
didn't yet know.

She soon found
herself lost
in a maze filled
with silent oaks
and dripping
roses. She felt
comfortable.
Perhaps you find
some strange
pleasure in getting
lost too.

Silence.

How sweet and charming.

And then she opened an eye
at the warning of her instincts.
She wasn't alone. She felt
her heartbeat in her throat.
Throbbing and sharp.

With the rhythm of her boiling blood, black clouds rose above the trembling trees and heavy winds began to blow.

And there she was,
in the center of the tornado.
All her animal fierceness.

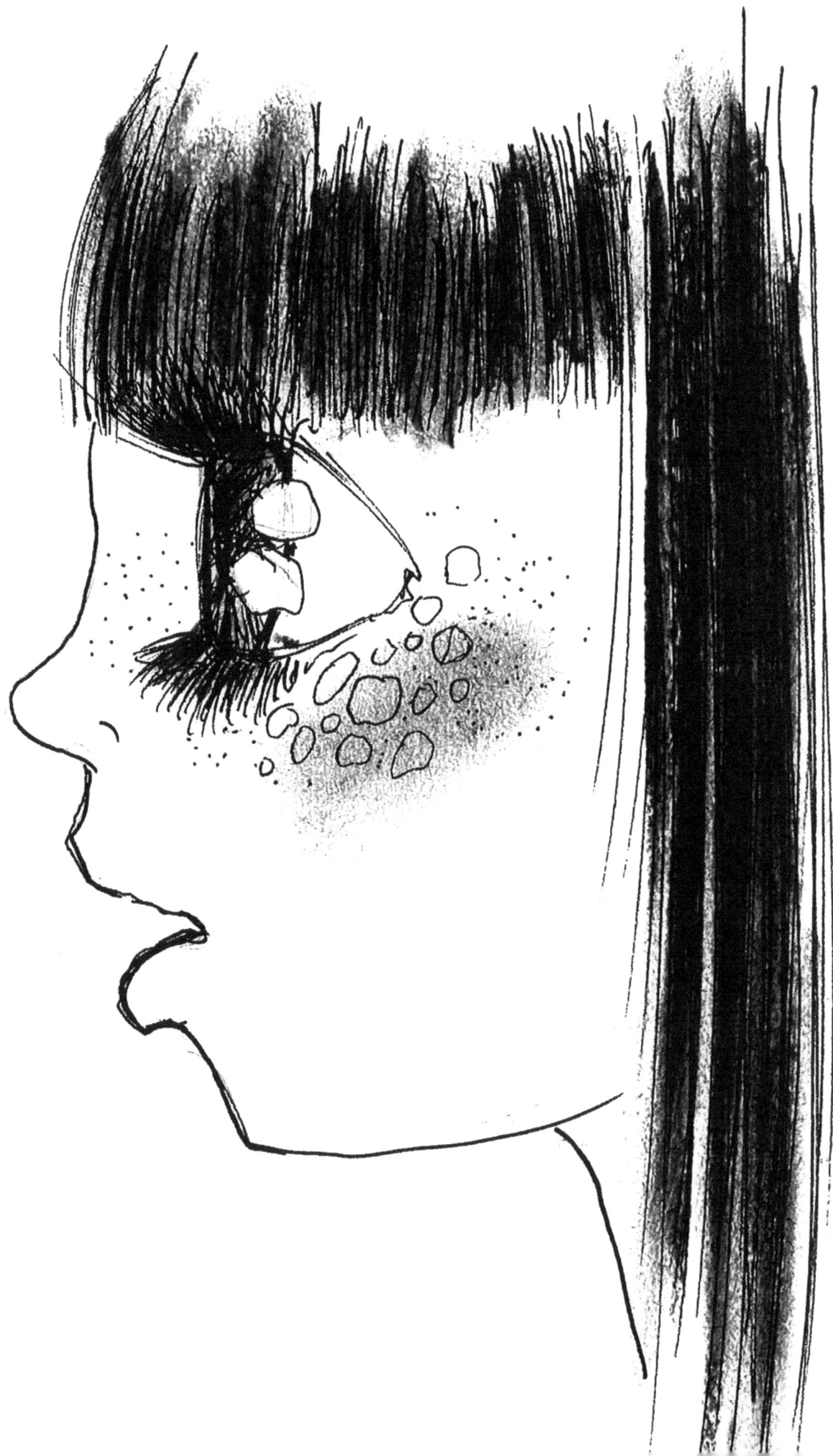

One sound
broke her
intense thoughts
into pieces.
What was that?
A howl.
She could hear
growling,
low and deep,
as something
came near.
The other animals
ran away.
They didn't want
to be there
when those beasts
collided.

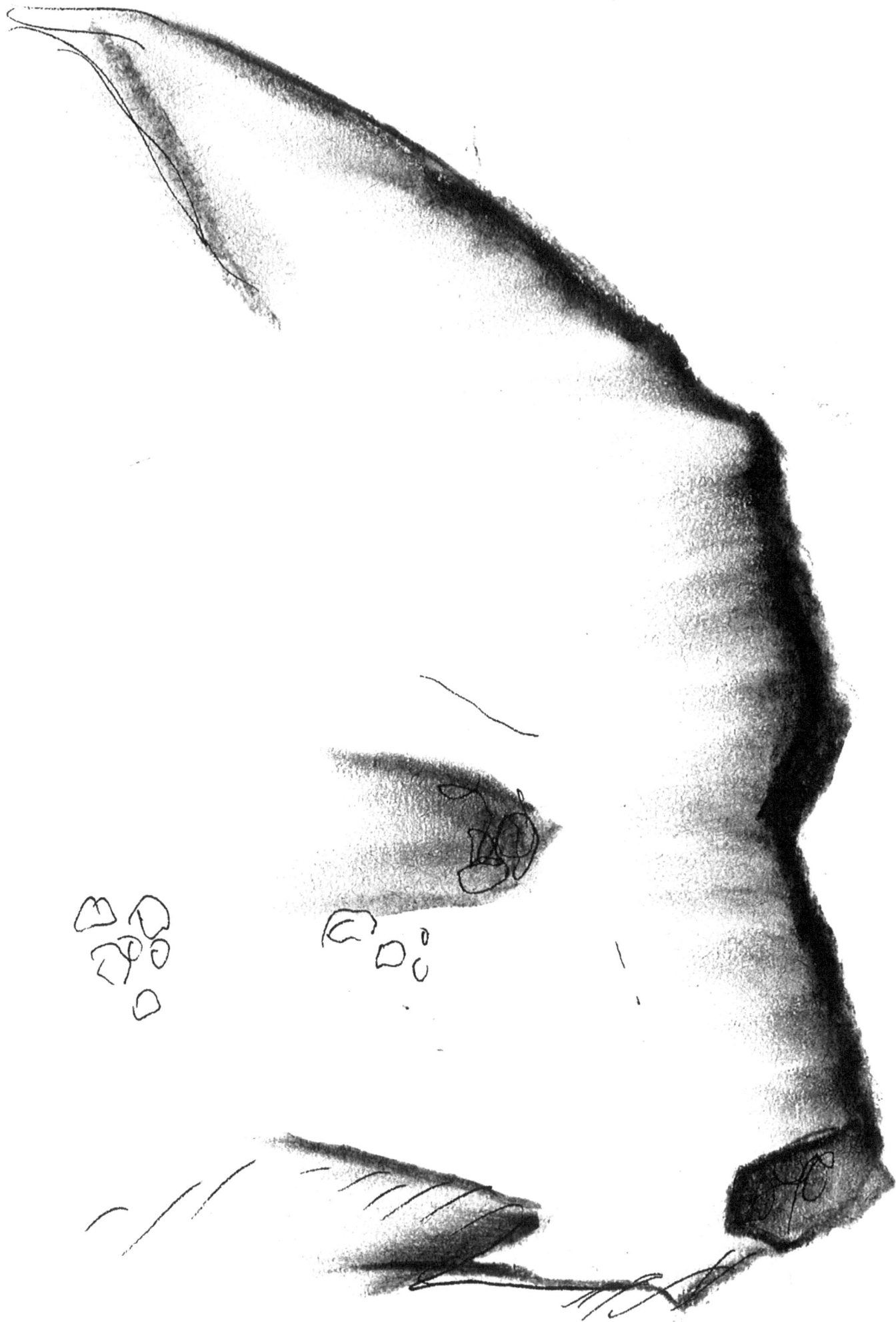

Every
palpitation
of her
heart
was like
a thorn
in her
veins.
He perceived
her trembling.

A roaring shadow
stood just in front
of her.

Breathing deep,
warm and fierce,
waiting for her
reaction.

She stood.
She looked him in
the eye.
A beast, a wolf.

The storm
melted above
them.
The rain
turned to mist
and the wind
died.

They were soaked and the fresh
smell of wet grass surrounded
them.

For her, it was
the first time someone
had stopped the
madness
in her mind.
For him, she was
the first one
brave enough
to face him.

She stepped toward him,
until she
was so close
his warm breath
blew her hair.

"How did you find me?"
she whispered.

"What's taken so long?"

They walked uphill
until they came to a view
of the mountains.
He stared at the landscape,
and so did she.
"What is this?" she asked.
"Why did you bring me here?"

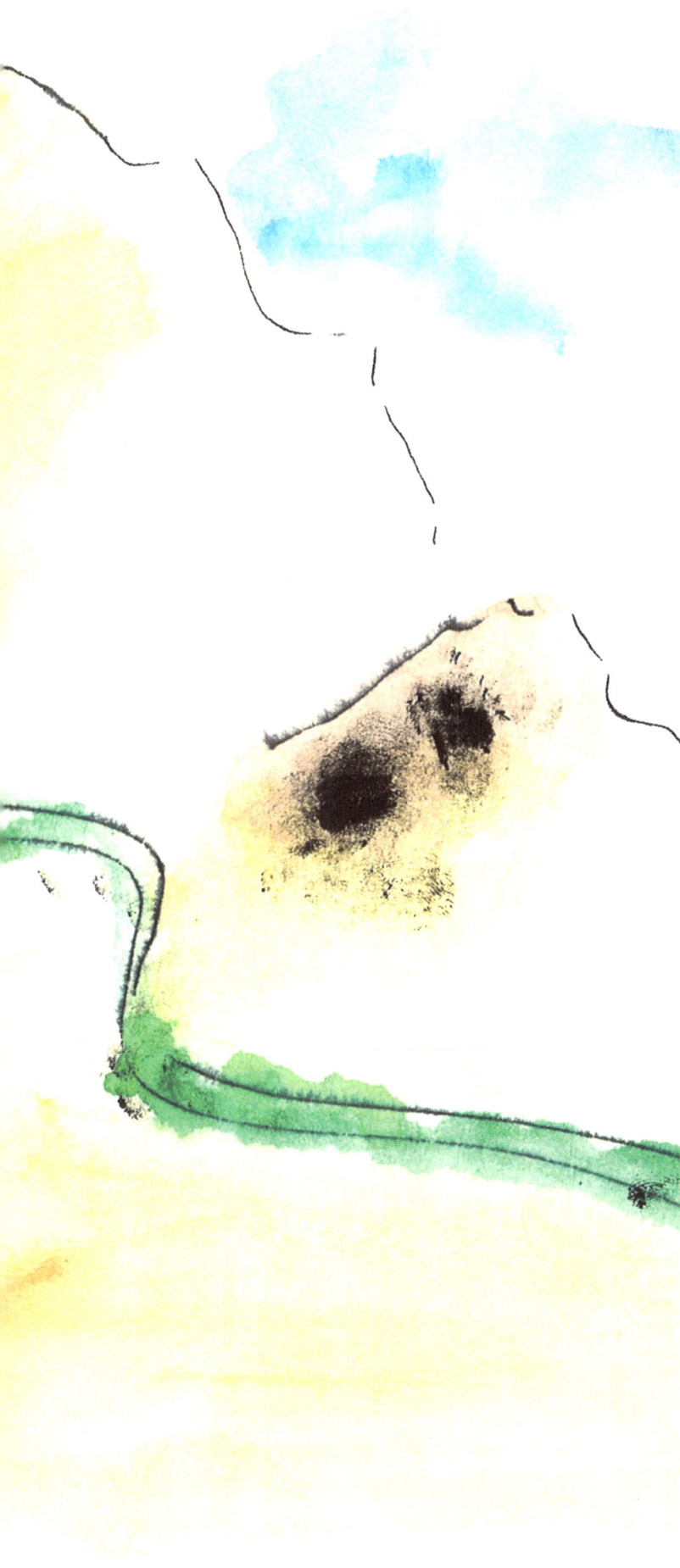

Something was
out of place.
Between the grey
and lonely
mountains, there
was a bright
little path,
covered in green
grass and bright
flowers.
She found it
beautiful, but
didn't understand
what it had to do
with her.

He nudged her to turn
her around. And she saw
that just behind her,
the path reached
her own feet.
It was following her.
It ended where she started.
That's how he found her,

finally.

By following the wild.

He had never had true
company, because no
one could handle his
fierceness. She had never
felt understood or been
guided through her chaos.
They were perfect together.

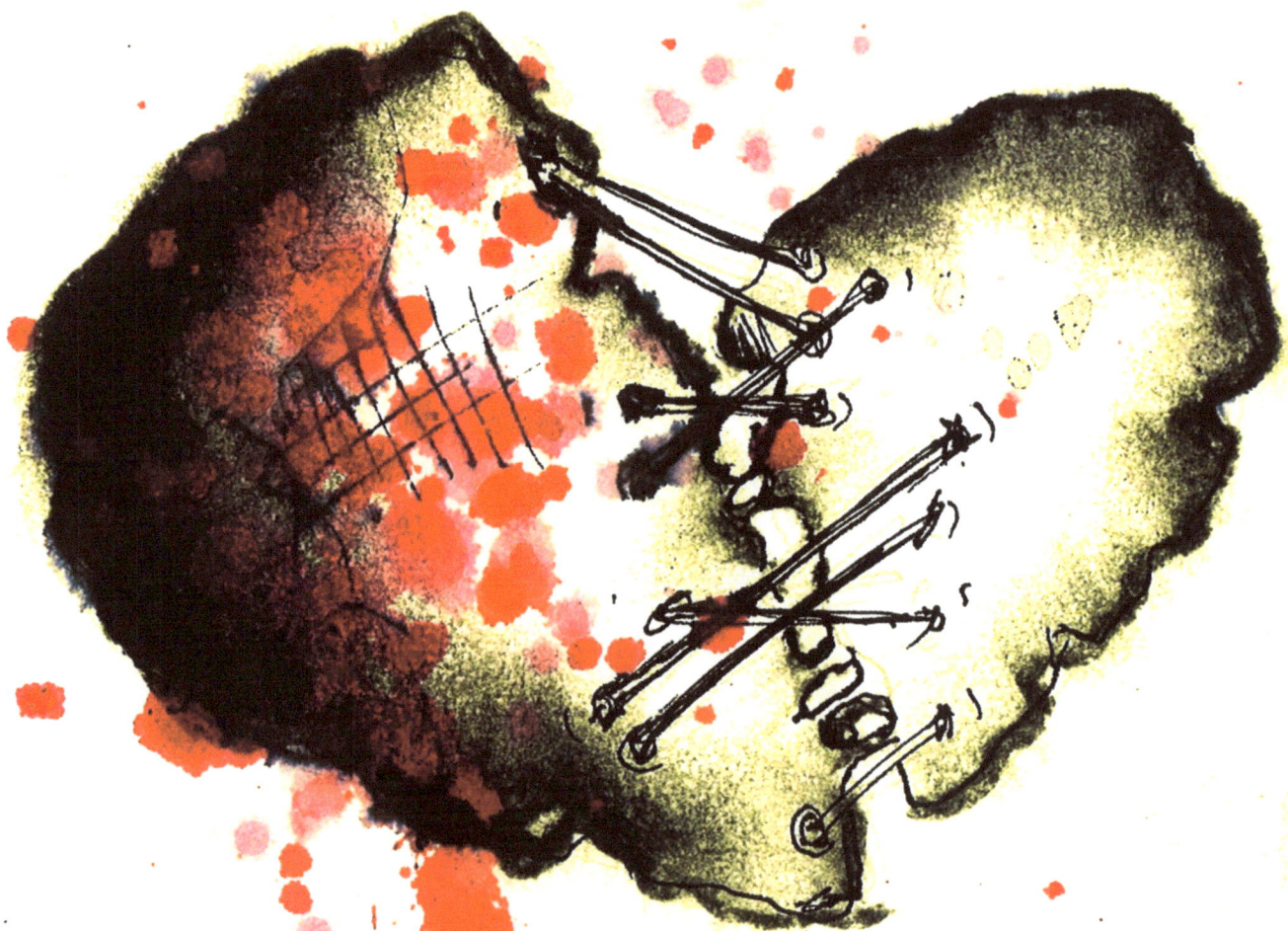

Sometimes, what seems a
burden is in fact your
highest virtue.
It takes the right person,
challenge, or situation
to show you just how
precious you are.
It may take a long time
to discover. But life will
give you a chance
to see it.

You are beautiful.

You are just perfect.

www.ingramcontent.com/pod-product-compliance
Lightning Source LLC
LaVergne TN
LVHW072108070426
835509LV00002B/66